Flowers Blooming Against a Bruised Gray Sky

Published by
Whit Press
Richard Hugo House
1634 Eleventh Avenue
Seattle, WA 98122
whitpress@aol.com

•

ISBN 978-0-9720205-1-0
Library of Congress Control Number 2003108242

Whit Press books are made possible in major part by the generous support of Nancy Nordhoff, Sherri Ontjes, our individual contributors and the following organizations:
• The Seattle Foundation
• Seattle Office of Arts & Cultural Affairs
• The Breneman-Jaech Foundation

For you all, our most heartfelt thanks and gratitude.

Welcome to the Hedgebrook Writer's Series

Hedgebrook is a retreat for women writers on Whidbey Island in Washington State. At Hedgebrook we believe in the power of radical hospitality—if you feed and nurture a writer's body, mind and spirit, and provide a quiet place where she can settle into the stillness of her soul—she will write to the core of her truth.

A day of writing at Hedgebrook ends in the farmhouse kitchen—where writers share a meal, their writing, their stories and the breakthroughs and roadblocks in their writing process. Over 1000 women have come to Hedgebrook since our founding in 1988, from across the U.S. and as far away as Zimbabwe, Thailand, Saudi Arabia and India.

At Whit Press we believe that assuring a place for women poets and storytellers to publish their work is an act of hope in action. It is grounded in the certainty that the written word transcends barriers of culture, race, and class, and intimately connects us to one another's lives—as individuals, as communities, and as a planet.

Both Whit Press and Hedgebrook are committed to connecting women writers with audiences worldwide. This annual book series is a physical manifestation of that vision.

Welcome to the Hedgebrook Writer's Series!

Flowers Blooming Against a Bruised Gray Sky

poetry by Uchechi Kalu

Whit
Press

1634 Eleventh Avenue   Seattle, WA 98122   www.whitpress.org

Acknowledgments

My life is a song of redemption and love. Many people have sung the chorus, and through them I know grace. You know who you are.

This is for my chosen family, especially my sister Sarah Zuniga, my brothers Michael Lamb and Trevor Baumgartner, and the beloved Gabriel Sayegh, for a steadfast faith that never wavered.

This is for Ruth Forman, for paving the way and for support and feedback.

This is for the Hedgebrook Cottages on Whidbey Island, for the space and time to write.

This is for Claudia Mauro at Whit Press, for believing in me and for the patience all these years.

This is for the Poetry for the People writing community at the University of California, Berkeley from 1997-2001.

This is for the late June Jordan, for everything.

This is for my blood family, without whom none of these experiences would be possible. Special thanks to my brother Emmanuel, for teaching me that loving and living is the same thing.

Grateful acknowledgement is made to *Revolutionary Voices,*"(Alyson Books, 2000) for publishing the poems "Affirmation" and "Tasting Home."

This is for my life, which was never a wrong move.

—U.K.

for all those who fall down and
find the courage to get back up again
and for June Jordan

Contents

Shedding Skin

Dancing with My Brother

Clash with the American Dream

Haiku I

Another Friday night
My mother cries from my father's blow
I watch the rain pour

I Wonder Where You Sleep Tonight

for my brother Emmanuel

Because I can't stop
dreaming of you
lying in your own blood and shit
with no teeth
to dress your smile

A hint of jasmine
reminds me of the coming summer
your face drinks up the sun
on those lazy Saturday mornings
just before I pull off your sheets
and tease you
awake

But I wonder
where you sleep tonight
caught up in juvenile hall
back in another lockdown
after two months out
and I don't know
where to place my red eyes
in between periods and question marks
and even after two cups of chamomile tea
at one o'clock in the morning
I can't fall asleep

And you just turned sixteen
but no one in our family
lit candles
to usher in another year of your life
beautiful boy
I want you to smell the summer sky
I don't want to dream of you
lying in your own blood and shit
with no teeth
to dress your smile

I don't want to touch glass
the next time
I see your face

I Wish You Survived Too

for Sherrice Iverson

On the bathroom floor
of our Texas home
my eight year old legs
spread open wide
as my older brother
slams my head
against the tile
just before he pulls down
my Sesame Street shorts
and interferes with my right to dream
of hopscotch days and polka dot dresses

When he leaves
I try to clean the blood and sweat
off the floor
watch him walk away
and pray
for God to forgive me
over and over again

In a bathroom stall
of a Las Vegas casino
a man
three years younger
than my brother
rapes a seven year old girl
and interferes with her right to live

And I don't want to see any more
pictures in the paper
or hear any more
details of her murder

I just want to hold her hand
help her clean the blood off the floor
and ask if she too
loves Sesame Street

I Am Not a Political Poet

Let me be absolutely clear
you see I'm not a political poet
I just wake up every day
and Shell Oil is drilling
in my country
which means that
someone in my family will die
before turning 20
I do not have a theoretical understanding
of the global market
but when my cousin's belly is swollen
'cause he can't afford rice
and the price of the world's most dependable grain
just went up
I write
when my brother gets picked up by cops
who keep watch for his silhouette on our block
I write
'cause who wouldn't want their brother
sleeping safe at night
who wouldn't want the bombing to stop

Before obliterating each and every building
and the dead are my loved ones
who wouldn't want to put an end to globalization
instead of defend free trade
when it means the majority of third world women
will bury their children first

So I told you already
let's be absolutely clear
I'm not a political poet
but if you burn down my home
bulldoze my land
make me search for my mother amidst rubble
then call me the trouble maker
you bet
I'll write about it

House Arrest on Your 16th Birthday
for my brother Emmanuel

No cake/no nothing
not even a note of song
family act like you already gone

You on house arrest
mom and dad say you stay out
past curfew
you failing ninth grade again
so they got a court order
make cops memorize you/shadow you
If you go anywhere but school

And you no fool
since there ain't no cake
and none on it's way
you jump out the window
fly past older brother's steel bar fate
social service
and an April court date

You run
to your friend's house
'cause they remember
to light a candle
make a chocolate cake
with vanilla swirls
and sing to you

Even after Prop. 21

Today
I call you up
to celebrate 17 years
even after
daily drug tests
a new probation officer every month
and those nights you stagger to your bed
with bloodshot eyes
you refuse to open your mouth
when mom and dad ask to smell your breath
even after all this
you're still here

Now mom says you give her
a reason to smile each day
you ain't failing ninth grade again
you're trying to go to college
make sure you don't end up
like your older brother
crouched over in a cell
where wheelchair blues
dictate his days

Today
I call you up
even after Prop. 21 passes by 65 percent
Pete Wilson wants to put brown boys in prison
before they can spell penitentiary

This poem says
steel bars and cubicles
will not replace space ship star shooter
bunk beds and NFL flannel sheets
This poem says yes to your laughter
like the sun peeking over the hills
after days of rain

I don't want to hear your voice crack
every time I call you

This poem says yes
to the details of your life
that will help you
till the soil
and grow grass
over concrete and barbed wire

Clash with the American Dream

Momma tells me
work hard in school
earn a 4.0 GPA
so I can ace this country

I do not believe her
because momma
smart like me
works in a nursing home
stoops over someone else's toilet
earns six dollars an hour
with a masters degree

Today I Take Back My Name

It Won't Happen Again

An eight year old girl
draws imaginary playgrounds
in the sky
her eyes drift
anywhere but
between her legs
stretched open
and ploughed through
every day
after school

Now
she
wonders
what might have been
and could she have stopped it
but she doesn't want to spend time
using compound verb constructions
and question marks

If you ever
try to split
her land
or leave her
dangling
blood dripping
from her legs
she won't leave room
for questions
or possibility
period

In Response to Anyone
Who Thinks I'm Not African Enough

Sorry
I forgot
my spear
at home

I Am Tired of Shame

I have considered
slashing my wrists
slamming my fists
in someone's face
searching for a truth
a lie
a disguise
anything
but me

But I have also considered
stripping down naked
and looking
at myself
for longer than a minute

Yes
I have also considered
watching myself
stare back into my eyes
without shaking

Blowing kisses
to myself
for hours

My Angry Poem

If another white man
asks me why I write angry poems
I'll ask if he was listening at the last reading
I'll ask if he heard
the poem about petunias or daffodils
or your eyelids closing next to mine
on the first day of summer

If he still says
it's the way you read it
I'll ask if he heard the haiku
it was only three lines
and I even whispered
I'll promise
to wear brighter lipstick next time
maybe I'll try red
my usual purple darkens the mood

If he isn't angry about something
I'll ask if he's read the newspaper lately

If another white man
asks me for my number
after telling me I write angry poems
but I still look pretty good

I'll take his number
make him take me home
to mom and dad
and see if they think I'm happy enough
to qualify as his girlfriend
'cause he wouldn't want to carry anger
around with his cell phone and briefcase
on his way to downtown

When you
white man
ask why I write angry poems
I want to ask you if you think the president is angry
do you have to be angry to send planes to bomb and bulldoze homes
then apologize for the human casualties
caught in the crossfire
but I must remember that he is not angry
just diplomatic

It doesn't matter what I say
you've already decided that I fit the description
of an angry black woman
except in your eyes I'm a bit different
'cause I give you an erection

But white man
I'm working on it
meditating
asking the gods and goddesses
to help me release my anger
see there's yoga for anger
stress management classes for anger
meditation with green tea for anger
even bilingual classes for anger
so next time you come to the reading
I hope you can tell
I'm working on it

Affirmation

I be the one
momma always say
watch out for
be the reason my parents send me
to modeling school
make me a lady
who don't never want nothing
but a man

I be the one
who catch myself
looking at long black braids
and smelling apple plum perfume and you
I be the one not always lusting
after the big boys with beer bellies or biceps
'cause I be the one who like to choose

Be the one
who don't know
how to claim this song/afraid to write this poem
how do I/stop myself/from disappearing
when there ain't no word
to translate my kind of love
into the syllables that decorate grandma's tongue

Be the one make momma glance away
when my sister and I
strut down the hall
like a parade of peacocks
wearing daddy's suits
Be the one Congress try to legislate out of sight
'cause I just don't act right

I be the one
loving women/loving men
loving you/who love me
I be the one
and I can't put a certain face
to love
I can't negotiate
the tender curve of your spine
into a certain body frame
or carefully constructed gender identity

I be the one
momma always say
watch out for
be the one God don't like
be the one have to sit through
daddy's Sunday school lesson
about Sodom and Gomorrah
and how the Almighty burns them out of sight
when they just don't act right

I be the one
my parents want to act like a lady
who don't never want nothing
but a man

But I be the one
who be loving women/loving men
loving you/who love me
cause I ain't never gonna let nobody
tell me
to live
without love

They Came for Me

I am not wrong. Wrong is not my name.
My name is my own/my own/ my own
                    —June Jordan

Somebody came for my brother
spilled his body across the freeway
so he never made it to 18

They have come for my mother's heart
sometimes she says she can't hear it beat
defeated from burying too many children

They have come for my father's smile
these days he wears a frown
clutching the Bible
reciting scriptures
instead of letting the river fall down his face
'cause he's supposed to act like a man

They have come for my older brother
car accident crushed his legs
dangling from a wheel chair
he only stares through steel bar cubicles
orange has become the only color
in his wardrobe
his skin burst open with blisters
guess the guards had nothing better to do
that morning

They have come for my family
they have come for my grandmother
never made it past forty

gave birth to nine kids
only 2 survived
only one is alive
my father
gave birth to me
and I still walk this earth

They have come for my body
grazed the land between my thighs
looking for gold/diamond/oil
while I toil/bend my back
to fill their mouths

Yes
they have come for my body
fault lines etched across my back
my stomach a hollow grave
to bury everyone else's blame
take on everyone else's shame
instead of singing my name

They have come for my ovaries
cysts hoot and howl
dance across my belly

They have come for my smile
the one thing I took back from my house
didn't let my mother's reminders

to keep my mouth shut stop me
maybe she thought
this crumbling city of teeth
held nothing but ruins

They have declared war on my people
my spirit
sometimes it's my family come to take
sometimes it's my government
come to take
sometimes it's me come to take

They have come
to offer you Big Mac meal deals
a four wheel drive
Visa/Mastercard
a big back yard
but I don't need this
I've got my smile
that I won't hide anymore
my lips will not wait at the door
I will not be your safari getaway
African queen
I will not let you tour
my land/my people
I will not let you spread
my legs open and drill

I will not become your Shell Oil whore
'cause if and when you come
I will come
take what's mine

'cause I need my smile
my cotton pillow hair
the way I stare at anyone
who looks my way
I need my sweaty palms
my crooked teeth
my bone black hair
I need my lips
my voice
my choice
to love anyone I please
to tease you
with the possibility
of coming home with me
I need my laugh
my full belly ain't gonna swallow your shit anymore laugh
my devastating/contemplating
what to do about the next tragedy
in my life laugh
my lazy Saturday morning
with you in my arms laugh
I need myself
I need myself
I need myself
I need myself whole
I need myself whole
I need myself whole
speak in tongues to my face
saying no to disgrace
I need myself whole
I need to rebuild this city
and begin again

When Poetry Ain't Enough

You can tell me racism doesn't exist
but you can't insist that the cops
didn't stop my mother
pull her out of the car
handcuffed to the concrete
to remind her she's one of the few
black women
in this town

You can tell me homophobia
doesn't exist
in San Francisco
but you can't tell me that even in
San Francisco
I didn't hear the brother on the corner call me a *fucking dyke*
as I held my lover's hand that night
you can't tell me that as he followed us
I didn't think that he just might corner us into
an alley and stain the sidewalk red with our lives

Go ahead and show me statistics don't mean much
they're just numbers and how can I be sure it's true
1 in 3 black men in prison or on parole
they end up dead or locked up
under the watchful eye of the state
try and debate
tell me they don't qualify for endangered species status

I'll show you my younger brother's tombstone
maybe you can hear my older brother moan from his cell
see you can't opinionize
strategize or theorize my truth
my blood
my story

'Cause I know what I've seen
where I've been
whose dead
whose among the living

Regardless of what any ivy league degree
taught you about my people and my kind

You can tell me that World Trade Organization
and international policy is doing the best it can
for the third world

But you can't tell me that someone in my family isn't dead
'cause there was nothing to eat for days
and filling coke bottles at the plant
can't pay enough to feed a family
of seven

This is my poetry
you can't find it in the newspaper

This is my poetry
you can't debate the facts of my life
pretend it didn't happen
imagine things different

And I'm tired of complaining
about history books leaving me out
this is the poets responsibility
to document
and tell the stories

No it can't pay the bills
fill the gas tank
or even bring my brother
back

But it can rewrite history
and leave a mark
no one can erase

Poem to the Brotha Who Said "I Like Your Poetry, but Don't You Think It's Kind of Intense."

This goes out to women
who've been told
you're too intense
'cause you walk down the street
ready to practice your new moves
you learned in self defense
at night
or in broad daylight

This goes out
to anyone who's been told
you're too intense
a.k.a. too difficult
got too much drama in your life
you could start your own one woman show
I'll bet you've heard that before

or what about the woman
on the corner of 24th and Mission
brothas whistling and wishing
you could be their mama
even if you haven't finished high school
and don't plan on taking care of anyone
after growing up with eight brothers and a father

This is for the way
you strut
down the street in the shortest skirt
and give them the hand when they talk to you

This is for the way you wince
when they say
ok whore
I don't need you anyway

This is for anyone who's ever been called
tragic
like the Greek play
like your life is a stage
like you want to set up a podium
and say
hey everybody
this is my life and it's so damn sorry
tickets are selling quick
so please reserve yours now

and yes this is personal
this is about being called too much
and over the top
and depressing
and overwhelming
and did I say bitch
or tramp
or skank
or what about our mother's words
girl whose too proud to close her legs
*una mujer sin verguenza**
the shame of the family
the demise of the civilized
the obstacle making the white man
see us as anything but pagan
and blasphemous
what about words like dishonorable
to make us sound like we burned down someone's home

and I'll say it again
this is personal
but before you use a word
make sure you know its' full meaning

I have done my research
and this is what I found

According to Webster's Dictionary of English Usage
intense means
Tending to feel deeply
Deeply felt or profound

So
to answer your question
Brotha
yes
I am intense
I am proud
I am in search of anything meaningful and beautiful
that you can't find at a Clinique counter

I am living in a world where the media wants me to think
I might find happiness in a red #4 bottle of hair dye and the latest
Gucci bag
or maybe if that doesn't work I should try finding myself a man
a real stud
in the army
where he can be all he can be
including the father of my baby
even though he just raped a third world lady

I am living in a world where
girls start hurling up their lunches after school
because somebody told them beauty came in dress sizes
and hair dyes and body buffing creams and lip plumping machines
and what about the breast implant
and Botox injections before turning twenty-one

With all this to do and make it to school or work each day
who has time to be intense
to watch the nightly news and mourn for the last baby
buried in a single village
instead we shrug our shoulders and say

that's the way it is
war brings casualties

Who has time to pay attention to the heart
except on Valentines Day
or when your cholesterol level is too high
from all those blueberry muffins for breakfast

I want to feel deeply
I want to close my eyes
run my hands across your forehead
and say *I love you*
instead of *you're kinda cool*
I want to think about more than men
and fast cars and too many drinks at too many bars

I want to listen to anything profound
which means that anyone saying it is thinking it
which means there are less women vomiting up
their guts in the bathroom sink

Without *intensity*
world leaders disappear whole people
we begin to define
a bombing as a consequence of an unavoidable action
we begin to shake our heads and
don't do anything to prevent it

Without *intensity*
the woman walking the streets at night
won't practice her best moves
at night
or in broad daylight

Claim the word
it means
you didn't give up
or give in
to the race haters
and war mongers
it means you called it out
straight up
just like that
even when someone said you were nothing more than a
freak
gold digger
slut
whore
liar
all words to mean that you spoke out
against the Head of State
or Supreme Court Justice
or civil rights leader
or third grade nice guy teacher
or even the holy water sanctified preacher
when he said it was all in your head
and you were just trying to bring a good man down
when you know you really wanted it

Claim the word
it means you're here
living
loving
because of
and in spite of
everything

* A woman without shame

Today I Take Back My Name

Today I take back my name
from America's desire to chew it up and spit it out
chew it up and spit it out
its African nature
to create an American name

Years ago
I chewed it up and spit it out
hungry for a name like Jennifer or Julie
anything but ooo-chay-chi
Lord, anything but Uchechi

I let teachers/friends
chew it up and spit it out
I let them say ooo-cha-chi
I let them say cha-chi
I let them say
anything but ooo-chay-chi
Lord, anything but Uchechi

Today I boast
the beauty of my name
but when America told me otherwise
I believed it
until the sting burned so bad
that I put Africa back into my name
and I won't go back

My name is Uchechi
would you like me to spell that?

Tasting Home

When I Come Home to You
for my grandfather

When I come home to you
I will greet you in our native tongue
instead of bowing my head in shame

When I come home to you
no more dodging each other
in open alleys
on village streets

When I come home to you
Igbo words will fall from my lips
like spring rain
after a long dry season

When I come home to you
I will take you by the hand
walks into Ohafia's streets
know that uwa means earth
and we will dance
to the rhythm
of the rain

Perfect Morning Tanka
for my brother Emmanuel

Each morning
I rise
add sugar to my coffee
just a touch of milk
so I do not forget
my little brother's brown eyes

Remembering Home
for my sister

100-degree Texas heat
the ceiling fan spins endless
even the lemonade
can't cool us down
so my sister and I
fly out of the house
dig our feet into the dirt
and draw circles
with our hot pink and green toes

We talk about the new boy in class
we want him to look at us
like he stares
at all the white girls
so we practice
running
our hands through
our hair
dry and thick like sagebrush
we want the wind to blow it back
when we run

After that experiment doesn't work
we chase the ice-cream man
listen for the faint bell
urgent
like momma calling us in
for dinner

We empty our pockets
and carry our feast
down the street
I eat a snow cone
while my sister sucks on a lollypop
her tongue bursting red
like a pomegranate

When we feel satisfied
we lock arms and make our way home
We crawl into bed
we pretend to lie in
the Grand Canyon

Our laughter fills the night air
even when dad warns us to stop
we continue

Our voices constant and certain
like crickets chirping
after the summer sun
goes down

My Grandfather's Crackers

My grandfather
keeps a box of British crackers
under his rust iron bed frame

When you visit
he pulls them out
like a trophy
he peels off the plastic wrap
like a mother
unfolding her baby's blanket

While we eat
I don't think about
how the stale pale taste
sours my taste buds
or wonder about the expiration date
because with each bite
his eyes glaze over
he tilts his head back
and paints his past
with the flutter of his lips
he shows me rows of cornfields
pressed into hard worn hands

I imagine
a young man
in a soldiers uniform
dressed to impress my grandmother
enough to marry him

With each bite
his hands tremble
just like mine

He offers me another
after another
each bite
a passage into his world
he wants me to chew slow and swallow
so when the earth takes him home
someone else can tell his story

Rain

Summer sun sets
across red clay soil
stretches into the river
where children laugh
and fetch water to carry
home

I watch them
from the window of my grandfather's house
their legs bob
and bodies swerve like ostriches
buried under the weight of buckets

My first trip home
since I learned how to walk

Tonight
rain runs down rooftops
this
our music for the evening
while grandfather talks in Igbo
a language my parents only whisper
behind bedroom doors
since we came to America

Now
he wants to recite the past 18 years
recreate my life in his own tongue
and I need to call my mother
from the next room
I want her to break down these words
for my deaf ears

We travel back
ten, twenty, maybe thirty years
his 4'10" frame
each muscle still strong

Callused hands cover mine
sculpted into an oak tree
from too many bent back days
planting cassava and corn

Maybe his hands can show me
where the soil meets the river
even though I don't know one thing
about that river

I don't need to call my mother
now
as his lips tremble
I can see rows of cassava
in the creases of his hands

And I want to call Nigeria
my homeland
but I don't know how
to bring back
the sound
of rain on rooftops
with the parting
of my lips

Nigeria 1967

History books never talk about
Nigeria 1967
the year Igbo children
traded playgrounds for bombs
and how our people fled the north
when the government burned villages
our homes crumbling
in the palms of our hands

My parents never talk about
how my dad slept in bushes
with a gun at his side
or how my mom
spent her high school days
treating burns caked over
like cooked sugar
while trying not to take sides
over who should live
and who should die

And all the politicians say
we should move on
put it all behind us
and form a new country
even though one million dead
our villages still smell of bombs and blood

Our children's ashes
have become the altars of our homes

Who will build new houses
and bring back our playgrounds
who will bring back our poets
their words buried six feet below
our land

Who will remember Nigeria 1967
and tell my children
so that our stories become
flowers blooming
against a bruised gray sky

Haiku for Ohafia

rain soaks the village
children drench their skin
a morning shower

Tasting Home

for June Jordan

As twin babies
my sister and I
cross the Atlantic
say goodbye
to our African coast
in Igbo and English
until at two years old
our mouths dry up
like the desert
only cries of hunger
escape our lips
and no one knows why
so my mother lifts her eyes
to the sky
raises her hands
as if waiting for manna from heaven
to loosen her babies' tongues

The child psychologist
advises her to stick to one language
so my parents drop Igbo
only whisper it behind closed doors
like a secret

So I speak English only
sometimes pressing my ears
against my mother's bedroom door
hoping I can hear something/anything
to say at Igbo parties
so other teenage girls don't laugh
I speak English only
until my feet touch the red earth
of my Nigerian village

where Igbo words fill the rhythm of the air
and my lips dry up
my eyes can only stare
praying for God to loosen my tongue

Then you say
we should write poems in home language
Igbo words should dance across paper
never stopping until the beat of the song ends

Then words fall from my lips
through long-distance phone calls
asking mom how to say something/anything
to end this eighteen-year drought

Now
words fall from my tongue
like rain from the sky
and I am tasting home
for the first time

T'ang* Poems

* T'ang poetry is a style of classical Chinese poetry from the T'ang Dynasty.

A Message to Shell Oil
for Ken Saro-Wiwa and the Ogoni people of Nigeria

dig drill drain each drop
noose hang hope greed stop
child starve stare bare land
black life Shell cash crop

Poem for Amadou Diallo

night fall foot step creep
cop shoot blast life sweep
bow head turn walk pray
cry count dead black heap

How can we tell our children not to use violence?

child watch screen life still
stripe flag fly bomb kill
know house hide gun find
shoot friend watch blood spill

El Campesino*

bend back stoop work field
sun set night bring shield
crop grow stick prick skin
boss grin take home yield

*farmworker

The First Day of School in an English-Only Classroom

ink flow child write name
hear laugh cringe feel shame
bow head flood fill face
wipe tear smile play game

Poem after the Death of Matthew Shepard

wear heel strut dress drag
hear name call spout fag
feet move close rip skirt
grab gang rape choke gag

Homophobia

spread lip find mouth kiss
feet creep stop stare hiss
back tense eye swell flood
drop hand leave end bliss

T'ang for Palestine

tank drive plough crush land
grasp rock blood drip hand
child shriek steel pierce skin
hold head high flag stand

Friday Night at My Father's House

clench fist hit blood spill
hear scream pierce house fill
sweat stream stick damp face
lay quake shake life still

Love Poem

part lip tongue trace hip
taste cool breeze drink sip
sun set night come fall
flash smile wink heart skip

Stoplight

watch silk black braid sway
leg strut hip dance play
eye catch side glance look
hope red street light stay

Shedding Skin

Haiku V

Autumn will come
my sister's wedding
an arranged marriage

Low Tide

Today
I walk ocean floor
turning over sea shells
imagine your soft soap-smelling hands
on my face
your smile
the miracle of sunrise
but I can't find your hands
the color of this sand
so I wait
praying that this water
will bring you back
with the tide

Boys Will Be Boys
in response to my father

Boys need toys
a real live Barbie doll
to play with
so I lay with my legs open
as my brother discovers the intricate stitches
of my body
he unravels each piece
until I don't recognize myself
anymore

Poem for a New Immigrant
for my father

My father returns
from the immigration office
dressed like a Baptist minister
on Sunday service

His crisp blue suit
wears wrinkles
waiting for the INS officer
to call his name

His eyes stare at the ground
and we know not to ask
if he passed the citizenship test

Maybe he doesn't know every detail
about the Revolutionary War
and what if he skips a few questions
about the 32nd president
after 18 years of lost papers and files
traveling miles from Texas to Missouri
and now Massachusetts
after the INS searches through stacks
of misidentified permanent residents
they call his number

And he still doesn't know
the 32nd president
but he will come back again
because he wants to throw away
his pink plastic resident alien card
that knows him by an eight-digit number

Next time
he will tell them
everything they want to know
about the state of America
maybe then
they will call him
by his name

Ode to Quick Feet

Dad buys
a 56-inch 4-screen TV
he watches ESPN sports and the news
the only channels he allows
because anything else will make us lazy Americans
so we pray for a longer workday for teachers
we learn to move fast
and when the lock clicks closed
we scurry out of our holes
like rats
we watch MTV
our favorite station
we pull out the microwave popcorn
and root beer
and make a few hours
into a resort vacation

But when the engine roars
into the driveway
our eyes dart toward the door
like guerrillas at war
we position ourselves
on the boundaries of the living room
my sister watches the window while
my father's footsteps creep close

I say goodbye to Janet Jackson
return the remote control
to the couch
and smooth the creases
of the love seat
like a new dress

The jingle of the keys
makes my heart rate increase
so I fly up the stairs
make it to my room
pull out my favorite Ramona Quimby book
and pray for quick feet
next time

Ode to the Ice Cream Lady
for my mother

Sweat drips from the crease
of her head
her hands slip from the wheel
but she still drives
down city streets
searching for a baseball park
so she can sell her survival kit
for the heat

Chocolate cones/crushed ice
anything cold
and if you don't have enough money
she tells you
give me what you have
and I will make it enough
she counts it in front of your eyes
and like a magician pulls a rabbit from a hat
she does a monetary magic show

And on Tuesday
she gives out free Bazooka Joe bubble gum
so the kids with empty pockets
can coat their throats
with a taste
of summer sun
and save the wrapper
to prove it

A Prayer

I wake to find you
on the edge of the bed
the breeze blows back your shirt
the sun caresses your face
kisses your nose
sways from cheek to cheek
rests light on your lips
that I long to kiss

Black Boy in America

for my brother Emmanuel

What do I say
to my little brother
who spends an hour
reading every night
but still his teacher
puts him in the lowest group

What do I say
when he tells me
another white boy
called him *dirty nigger*
this time
his best friend

What do I say
to this wanna-be karate kid
high school football star
who can always outrun me
my brother
wants to go to Yale
work for NASA
and be the first black man
on the moon

What do I say
What would you say
to a black boy
not yet a man
in America

Always Laughing

I go back to Boston
to bury my baby brother
I stare at his body
his hair rests soft and snug
around his head
I sit through a wake and funeral
in one weekend

I come back to Berkeley
face tests/no time to rest
gotta be the best
and friends ask
why I don't go back home
or at least take a bath/relax

And as we stand drowning
in midday sun and sweat
I remember
my older brother rams his 4-wheel drive
right through me
he doesn't see
the stop sign in my eyes
and sometimes I feel like never moving again
sometimes I want to soak in
the flood that streaks down my face

But when I walk down the street
and see a smile
or a head tilted in my direction
I search for some affirmation
a testament to the blood that runs through
my veins

Because I find my brother
in every teenage boy
who wears his name in the back of his head
like a badge of honor

You see I made a promise to myself
and I don't need much to make it happen
I can get by on your smile
I can get by on your hand brushing my face
I survive
I survive
I survive
my lips pressed to the sky
drinking heaven's rain
and always
always
laughing

Ode to Your Lips

You part your lips
to trace the curve of my hips
a breeze blows in
from the window
and I see the clouds
move over
to catch our breath
steam dancing
through the night
sky

Haiku III

Clothes fill my room
reminding me of excess
wish they were blades of grass

After Writing a Poem

I take a bath
stay in longer
even if I have things to do
I let the water
seep into my skin
I begin to bathe
between my legs
wash away eight-year-old girl
shame
from too many sticky fingers
creeping up my thighs
I wash my breasts
cup them in my hands
and try to understand
that I am more than this body
I am more than these thighs
I am more than these breasts
I am this spirit
surviving

Haiku IV

light falls through window
your eyelashes curl open
the first sign of spring

Shedding Skin
inspired by Cornelius Eady

I know
what I have to lose
If I come out
      and say
what I mean

to say

I trip up
over rickety steps
      to get to the truth
the words not said

I do
             not think
I can
      take this sound
      to the tip of my lip
and blow it
        all out

When my father asks:
      Have you read your Bible today

I
      want
           to
               sail
over his words

and let him know that

after God
        and the Bible
I
still
don't
find   love

Arms spread wide
        open
in my house

falling apart/still
falling

After 20 years
        I learn
the value
of the words we whisper
behind closed doors

And how we don't mention
        the day
my parents
        found out

my brother
raped me
every single day
for over a year

And how do you put it all down
                or begin
to capture
the permanent change
on my father's face
when he walks in
to the same story
over and over again

                        Many people find it hard to believe that
after rape
after beatings
after burying my younger brother
after seeing my mother's face
split
from my father's hand

after

after the Bible does not save us

I still write
                about these things
running
                climbing

jumping

or whatever
                it takes

to translate
the hard words
of these rickety steps
under our feet

paying attention
to my inability
        to say
                something
anything

But I learn the value of saying nothing
                at all

and making up names
and places
places
I will never get to

I want survival
to find me
putting it all down
even if it means
I become
the words
we whisper
behind closed doors

Dancing With My Brother

I Celebrate Your 18th Birthday Without You*

lick lip whip pour bake
wrap gift spread frost cake
car screech life stand still
wave crash bring heart break

*My brother Emmanuel Kalu died in a tragic car accident on
February 25, 2001, one day before his 18th birthday.

To Write A Poem In Grief

What if you only know
the sound of verbs nudging
each other
to get out of the way
so each one can find
a space in your poem
to tell
stories

What if you've lost
the memory of action
what if you've stayed in bed
for weeks
and the only action
you remember
is sleep
weep
sleep
cry
do you pat yourself on the back
for remembering how
to rhyme

What if you try to use
synonyms
like sad
and upset
and sad and upset
because you can't think straight
and your loved one's not coming
back
and imagination and creativity
are like a new language
on your tongue

Do you remind yourself
that at least you've learned the value
of repetition

What if the only verbs
you remember
have something to do with
the way you lost that someone
what if pronouns and verbs
only dance together when you say
she died
she never came home

What if you can only live in the past tense
because you feel so uncertain
about tomorrow

What if sorrow
seems smaller than the smallest
cell block
what if the clock is ticking
for you too
and the mortgage is due
and you haven't checked the mail
in a month

What if this making of poems
starts with that first drop of blood
spilled
then smears across the page
of words
you can't seem to put on paper

Words muffled in your tears
words no one understands except
for you and God
What if verbs and nouns
don't know how to get along
wearing blue and red colors
claiming turf
waiting to occupy every square
inch of your paper
as if it were an LA intersection

What if you believed God
was a three letter word
for all the things
you can't explain right now
like the smell of your loved one's sweat
soaked in Calvin Klein cologne
on his favorite shirt
after football practice
like the memory of silence
Those moments of awe
The bird taking flight
the right kiss at the right time
the butterfly fluttering of the heart
the eagle soaring in the heavens
the death of Dr. King
the release of Nelson Mandela
the vaccine for polio
the baby who survived days underground
the lost love now found
the car accident that killed all
the car accident that killed none
t
The child that survived brain surgery
the child who died

before the first incision
the decision to leave behind
a six figure job
and handsome husband
for a plane ticket to anywhere
for a undetermined amount of time

The immigrant child who dreams
of more than McDonald's
and super-sized meals
the immigrant child who makes it to college
the one who fell to the ground
found with a bullet to the head
the one who just missed
a blow to the heart

The meaning under the words
soaking in your eyes
streaming down your face

The desire to believe
even in the face of nothing
to believe in

The things you can't explain
the questions you wish you could answer
the dancer
spinning in the air
twirling with this life
not knowing life was never there to catch you
and give you a soft place to land

After The Funeral

I want my brother sleeping
next to me
I want to tell him
I love him
over and over again
I want him to hear me
as his eyes close
lids fluttering like butterflies

I want him to know
that I can't walk through the men's section
of any department store
without seeing his face
I want him to know
that every black boy looks like him
sometimes I call out his name
hoping he will come running
home

I want to tell him
I have so many words and no place for them
to rest

I want to place flowers
on his grave

My Brother's Barbershop

When I need
a clean shave
I ask my brother
he gathers his clippers
like a chef
preparing a fine dine cuisine
he says he can
make us look like twins

He smiles
his eyes explode with laughter
like Fourth of July fireworks

He can't wait
to give me a fade
decorate my crown with lines
design each
smooth edge or crease
with just enough grease

I tilt my head back
and hear the bees buzz
around the halo of my head

He suggests we carve my name in the back
why don't we spell it phonetically
so no one ever mispronounces it again

After his 25-minute frenzy
we sweep up the forest
that gathers at the foot of my feet
stare at each other
in the mirror
his face
wears the weight of ocean waves
dancing at the tide of his eyes
that say
Uche
you look beautiful

The Dream Is Always the Same
for my brother Emmanuel

In my dream
you are still alive
here
next to me
breathing

In my dream
I lay in bed
instead of getting up
to face the day
someone knocks on the door
of my bedroom
and says
look who's here

You run
toward me
leap into the air
and land in my arms
slow and steady
like a crashing wave

You hold me
Uche
don't cry
please don't cry

Our arms refuse to let go
we hold on
laughing
laughing
laughing
we keep laughing

When you are here
next to me
breathing

I forget the car accident
I forget the news headline
I forget you died
the day before your birthday
I forget the shakes/the night sweats
the need to do laundry every week
'cause I've cried all over the sheets
I forget the hug at the airport
not knowing I would bury you
the next time we met
I forget to laugh
you taught me to laugh
no matter what
and I forget
because

I realize
You are not here
next to me
breathing

But you remind me:
yes
I am not here
breathing
but I am here
I am here
I am here

Against Abstraction
for my brother Emmanuel

I want to hold my brother close
bury my nose in his Kool-Aid–stained shirt
and smell dripping sweat

I want to bring back
Texas summers
we dance near the creek
our toes tease the grass
we walk to Seven-Eleven
to buy Reese's Peanut Butter Cups
and taste heaven
melt in our mouths

I want his breath
to cool my skin
I want to capture his laugh
in a jar
like fireflies glowing
through the night

I need to remember
the mole on his left arm
I notice it when he poses in the mirror
like a body builder
I remember him
I remember every detail
every time he said my name
like a line from a favorite song

I cannot afford to forget
the scar above his left brow
the pierced brow
I want to run my hands
across his forehead
and remember the day he tumbled
down the stairs
blood drowning the carpet
I need to remember

I must avoid every abstraction
every urge to describe
the color of his hair as anything but chocolate mousse
his smile nothing less
than the possibility of a clear sky
even with the chance of rain

I need to use my pen
with precision
because I cannot afford
to sleep without his name
dancing on the tip of my tongue

Why I Keep Going
for my brother Emmanuel

Because you tell me
tomorrow will come
with sunshine and jasmine
even if the forecast says
surely it will rain

Growing Up

I come home from college
to find your feet don't dangle
over the edge of the bed anymore
I have to stand on my tiptoes
to hold you in my arms

I watch you dress for a new job
and wonder if baking pretzels at the mall
makes high school girls call
our house like a 1-800 hotline

I eye the whisper of whiskers
that gather on your chin
you insist on showing me
the forest that grows in your armpits
you work out everyday
just so you can make the football team

I offer to take you to work
but you jingle dad's keys
I sit
so you don't see the ocean waves
breaking against the shore of my lashes

and you wonder why
my eyes meet the floor
you say you're just growing up
but police shot West African immigrant
Amadou Diallo 41 times
his body slumping onto his doorstep
just another black man
trying to make it
home

And cops won't hesitate
to stop your breath
because a tall black man like you
a tall black man drowning in his own blood
has become as ordinary and certain
as soldiers loading rifles
during target practice

Dancing with My Brother

Yesterday
I imagined us
dancing
on the beach
our toes tickling
each singular speck of sand
our hands held out
barely touching
fingers
your head tilted back
in honor of the moon
yeah
yesterday we danced
on the beach
but today
I stand here
watching the tide
come home
without you

"My writing, my putting my work out in the world is a non-negotiable thing."
—Uchechi Kalu

S. Renee Jones

Born in Abia State, Nigeria in 1978, Uchechi Kalu grew up in Missouri, Texas and Massachusetts. She is a writer, educator and performer who has taught writing at the University of California, Berkeley, high schools and prisons. Her poems have most recently appeared in *Revolutionary Voices* (Alyson Books, 2000). She makes her home in the San Francisco Bay Area. *Flowers Blooming Against a Bruised Gray Sky* is her first book.

http://www.uchechikalu.com

Colophon

The cover title type and interior headline type is set in Helvetica Neue, a font evolving from the original Helvetica designed by Max Miedinger in 1957. The name Helvetica is derived from the Roman name for Switzerland. It is based on the earlier Akzidenz Grotesk typeface (originally titled Haas-Grotesk) from around 1898. Helvetica became extremely popular in the 1960s and in 1983, Linotype released a retooling called Helvetica Neue (German for "New Helvetica") used here.

Text blocks were set in AGaramond from Adobe Type. AGaramond is a recasting of the classic serif type face Garamond, originally designed in the 16th century by Claude Garamond. Adobe AGaramond was designed by Robert Slimbach in 1989.

Interior stock is 50# EcoBook 50 by New Leaf Paper. Total recycled content 100%, post consumer recycled content, 50%. Cover stock is 12 point coated one side only with lay flat matt film lamination.

Book design by Tracy Lamb, Laughing Lamb Design, Jackson Hole, Wyoming. Images on the cover and interior are copyright free and were gleaned from a variety of image banks and adapted for use by the designer.

Print production by Sheridan Books, Inc. Chelsea, Michigan.

About Whit Press

The Literary Arts in Action. Support for the Independent Voice.

Whit Press is a nonprofit publishing organization dedicated to the transformational power of the written word.

Whit Press exists as an oasis to nurture and promote the rich diversity of literary work from women writers, writers from ethnic and social minorities, young writers, and first-time authors.

We also create books that use literature as a tool in support of other nonprofit organizations working toward environmental and social justice.

We are dedicated to producing beautiful books that combine outstanding literary content with design excellence.

Whit Press brings you the best of fiction, creative nonfiction, and poetry from diverse literary voices who do not have easy access to quality publication.

We publish stories of creative discovery, cultural insight, human experience, spiritual exploration, and more.

Please visit our web site **www.whitpress.org** for our other titles.

Whit Press and the environment

Whit Press is a member of the Green Press Initiative. We are committed to eliminating the use of paper produced with endangered forest fiber.